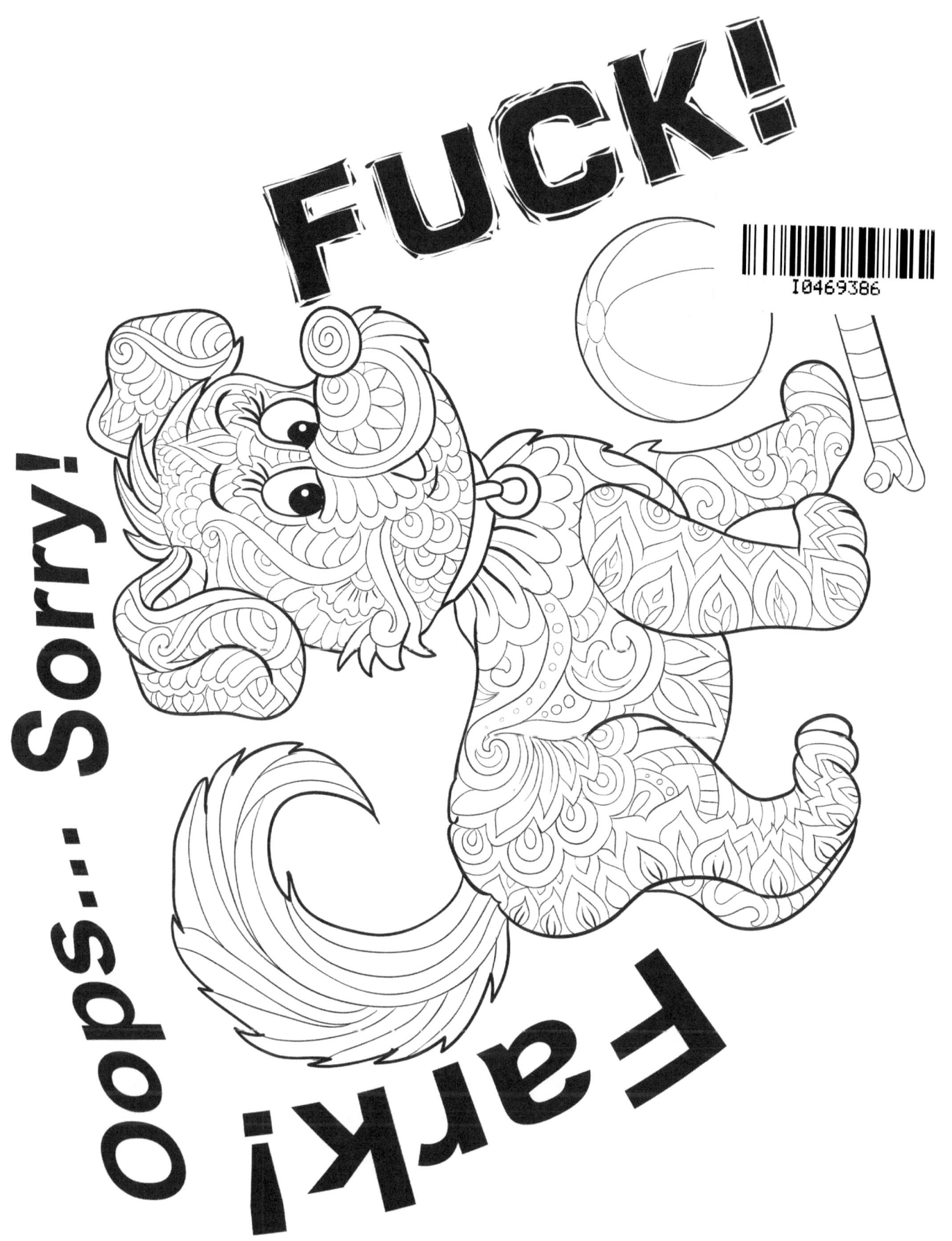

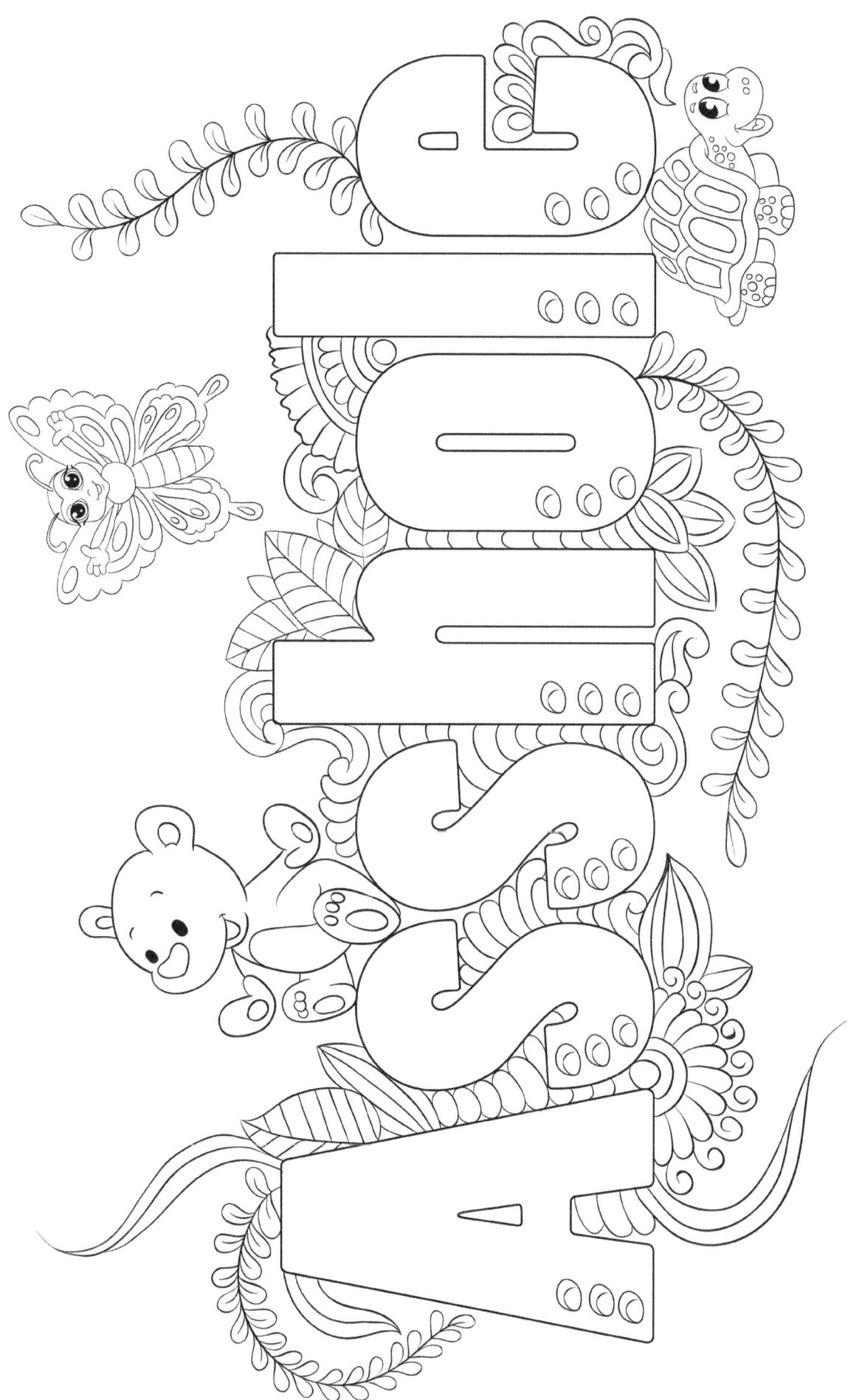

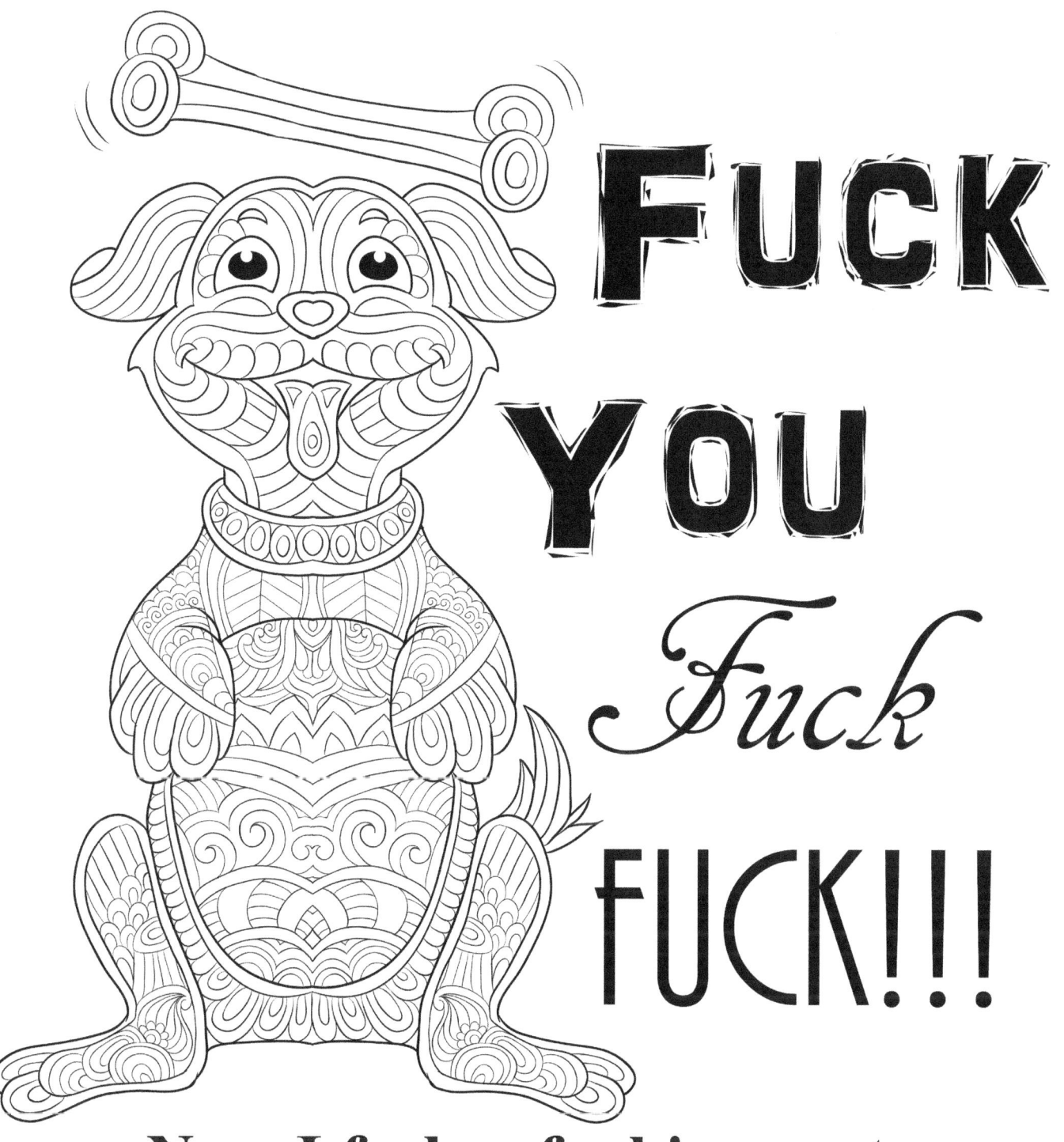

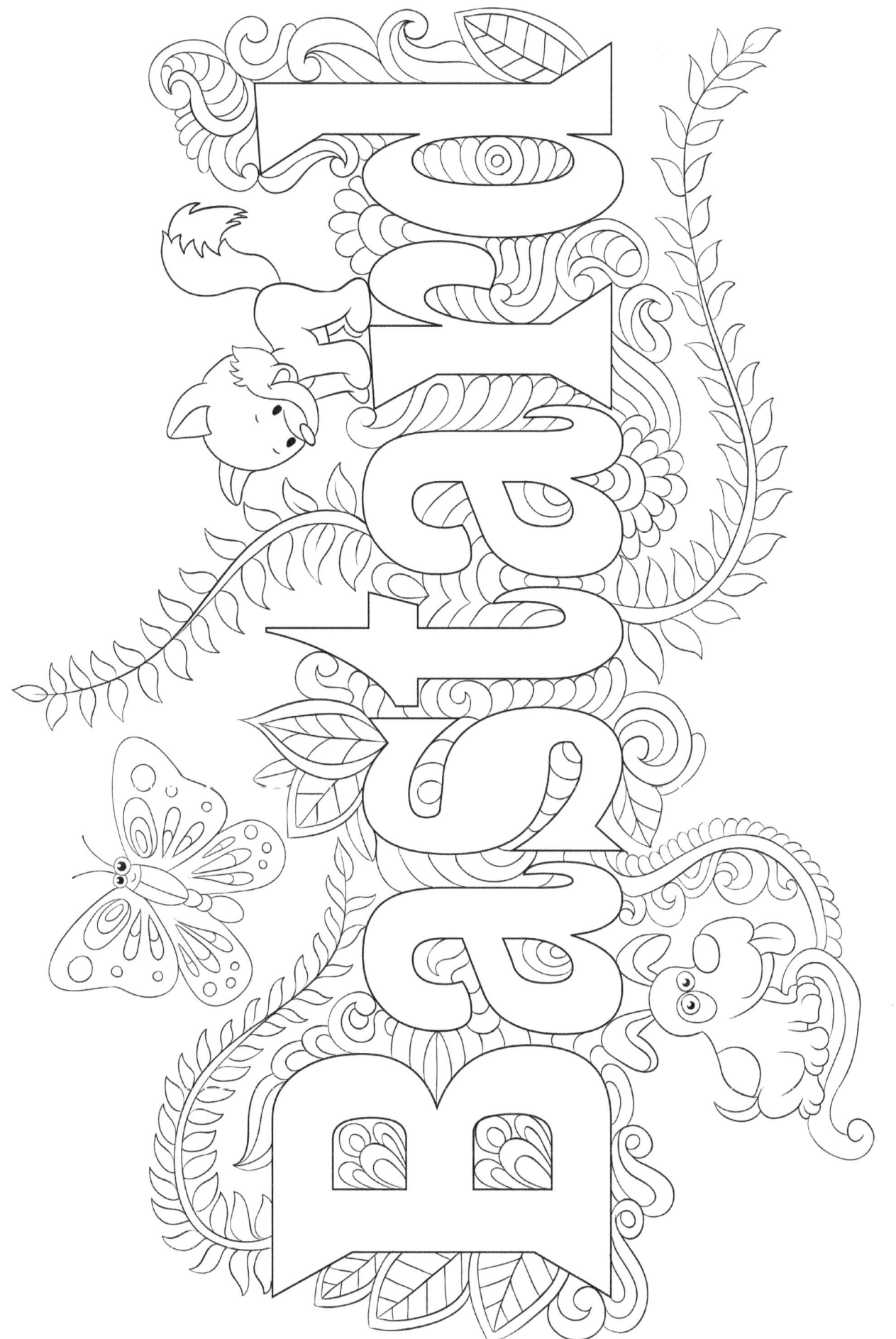

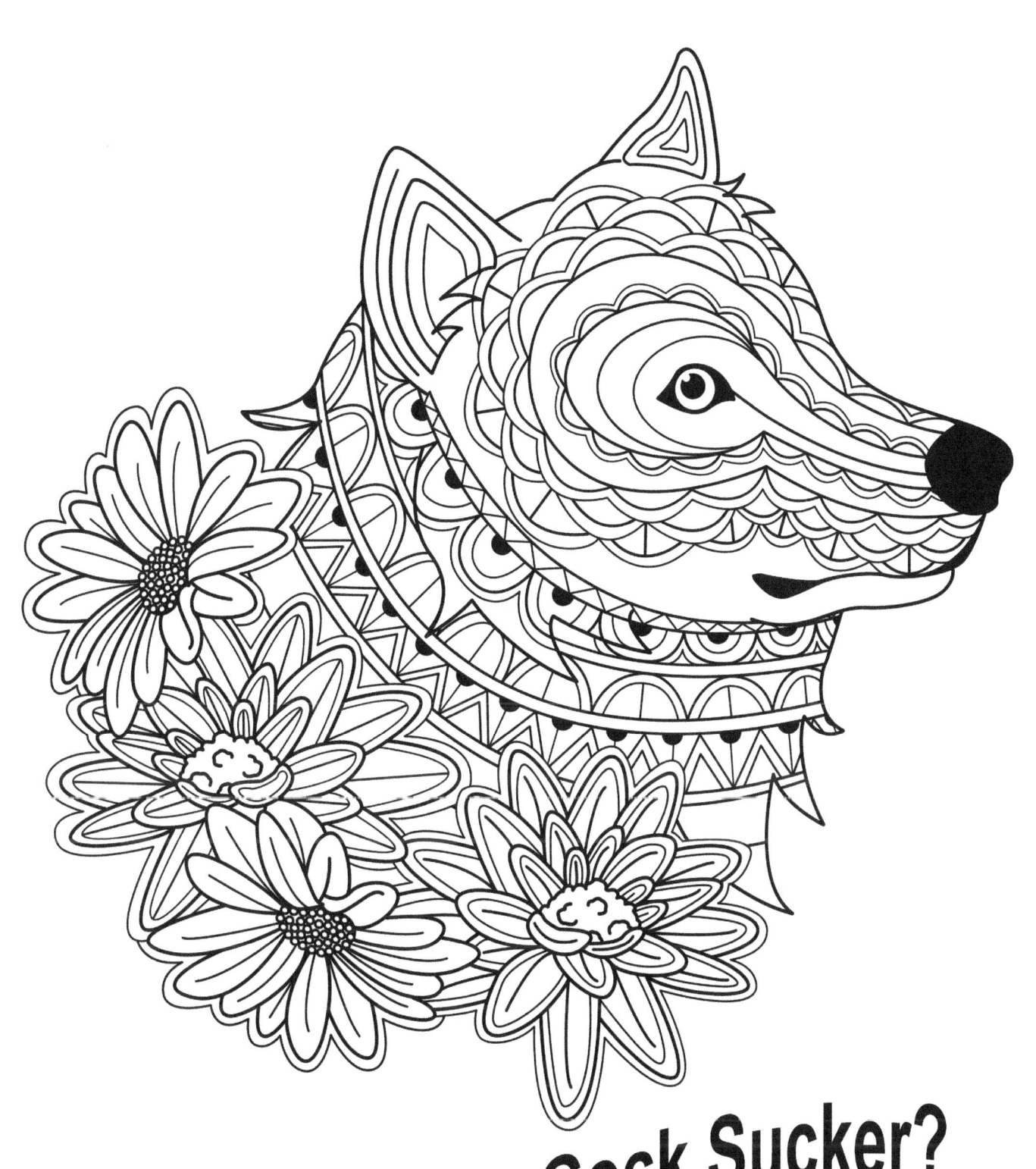

Motherfucker or Cock Sucker?
Pick Now...

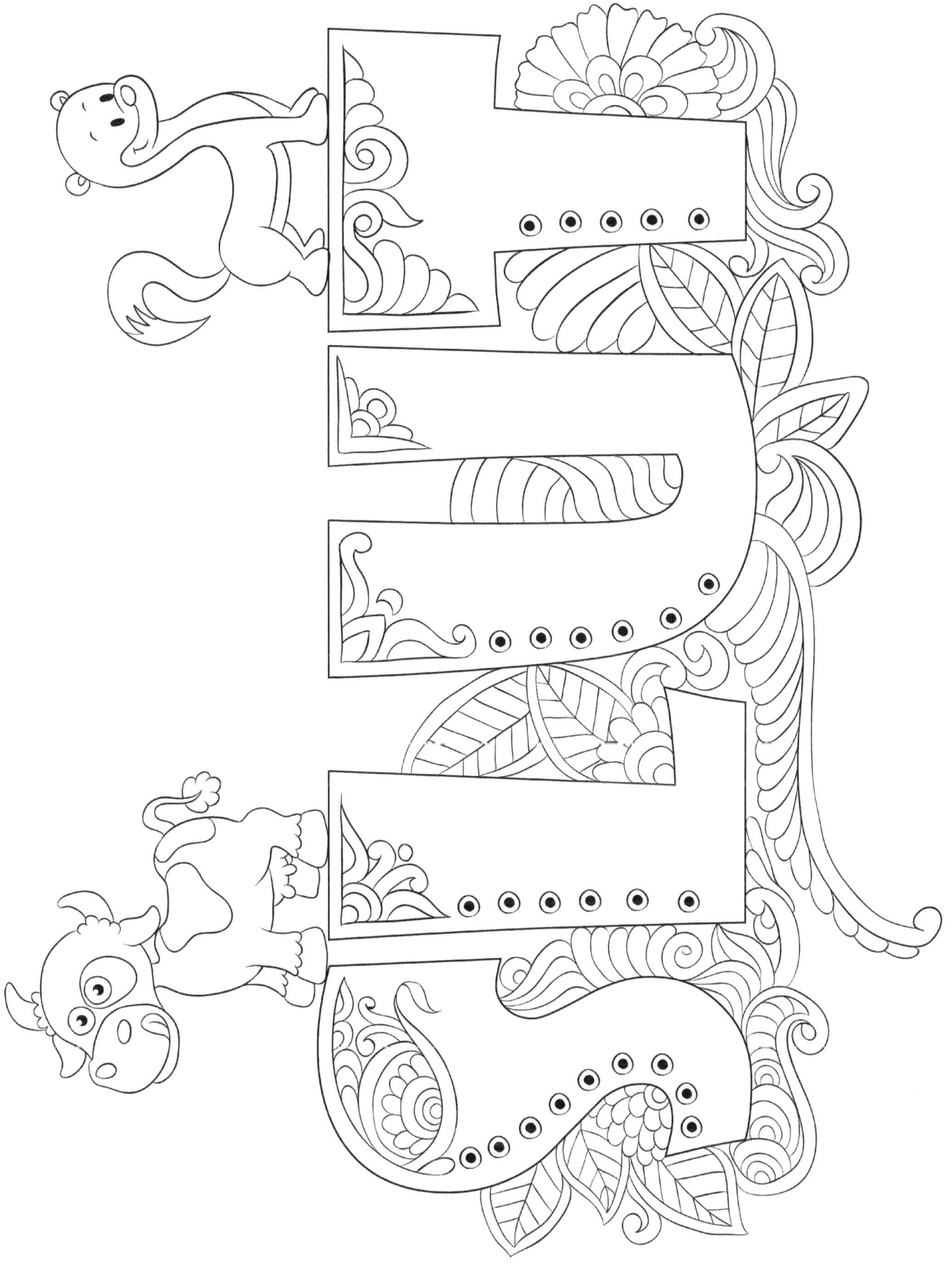

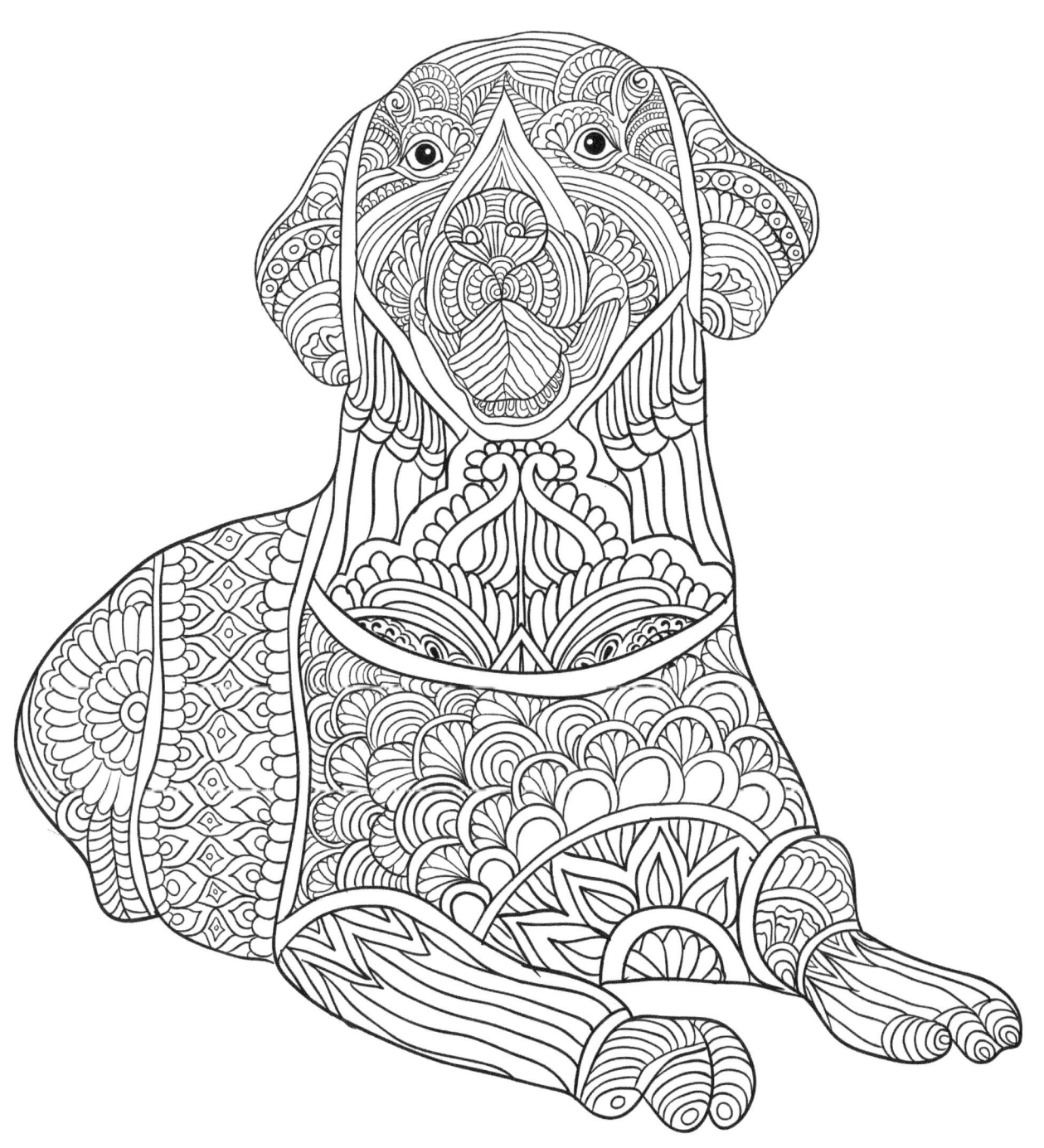

Shitballs, You Cock Jumper!

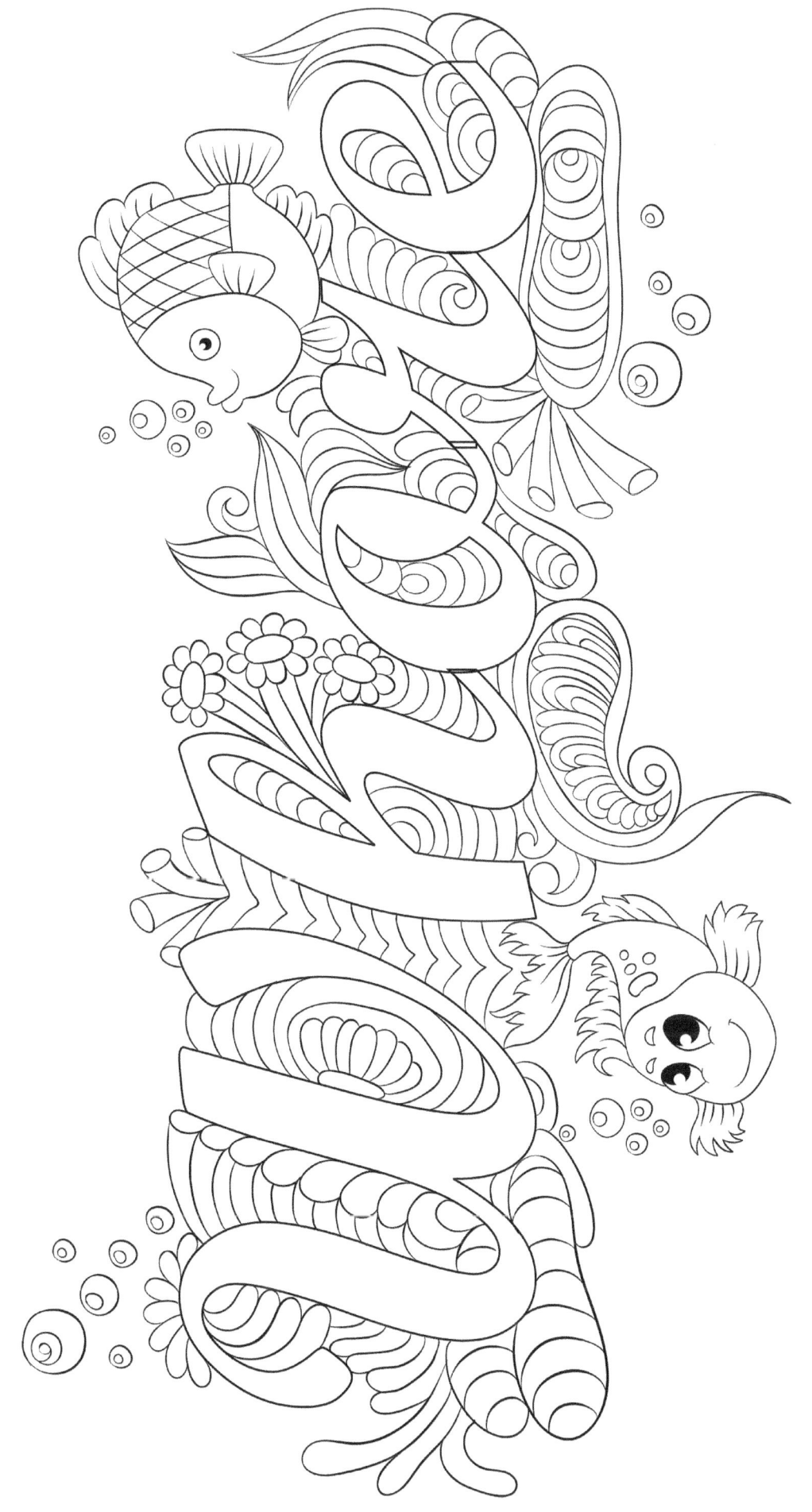

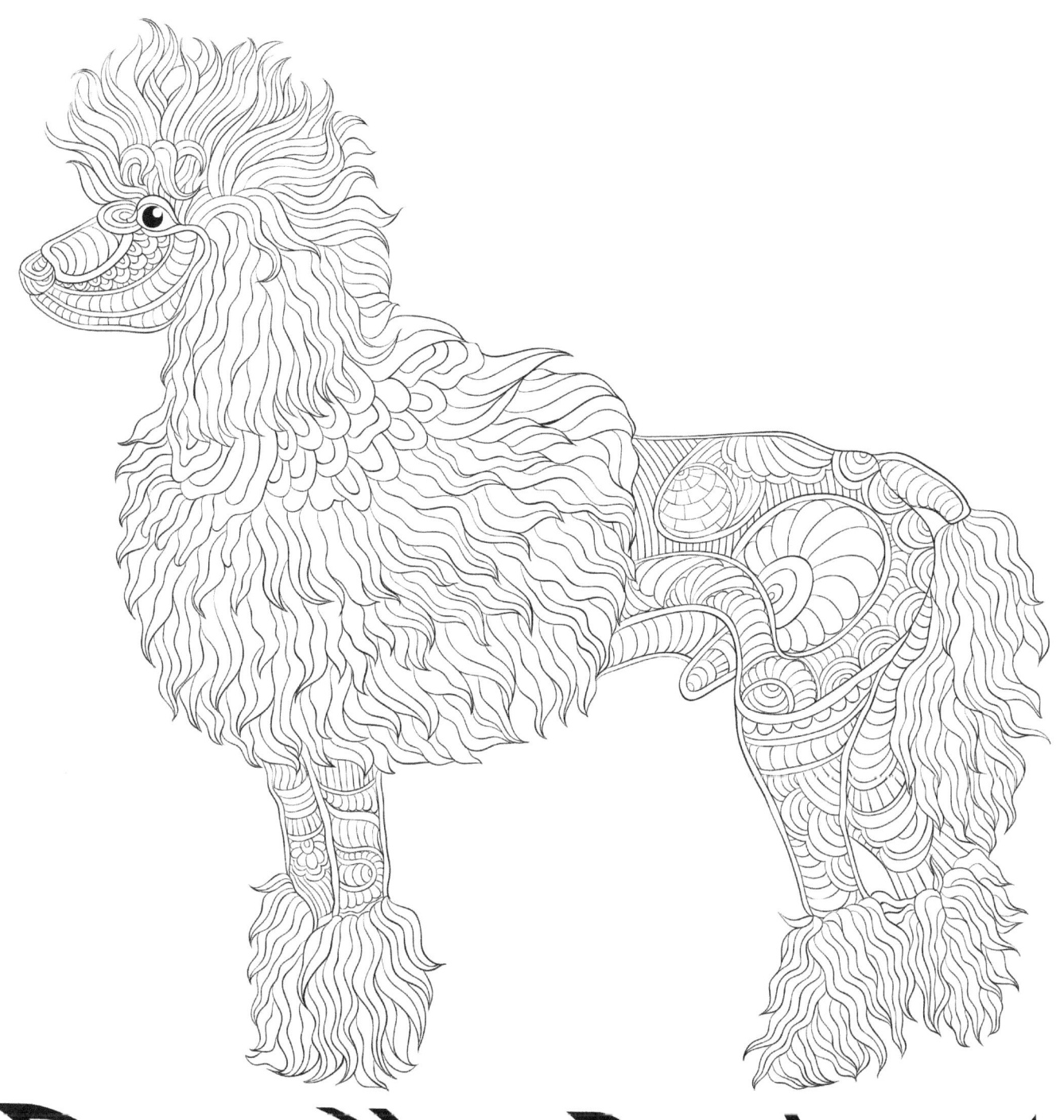

Damn You, Dumbcunt.

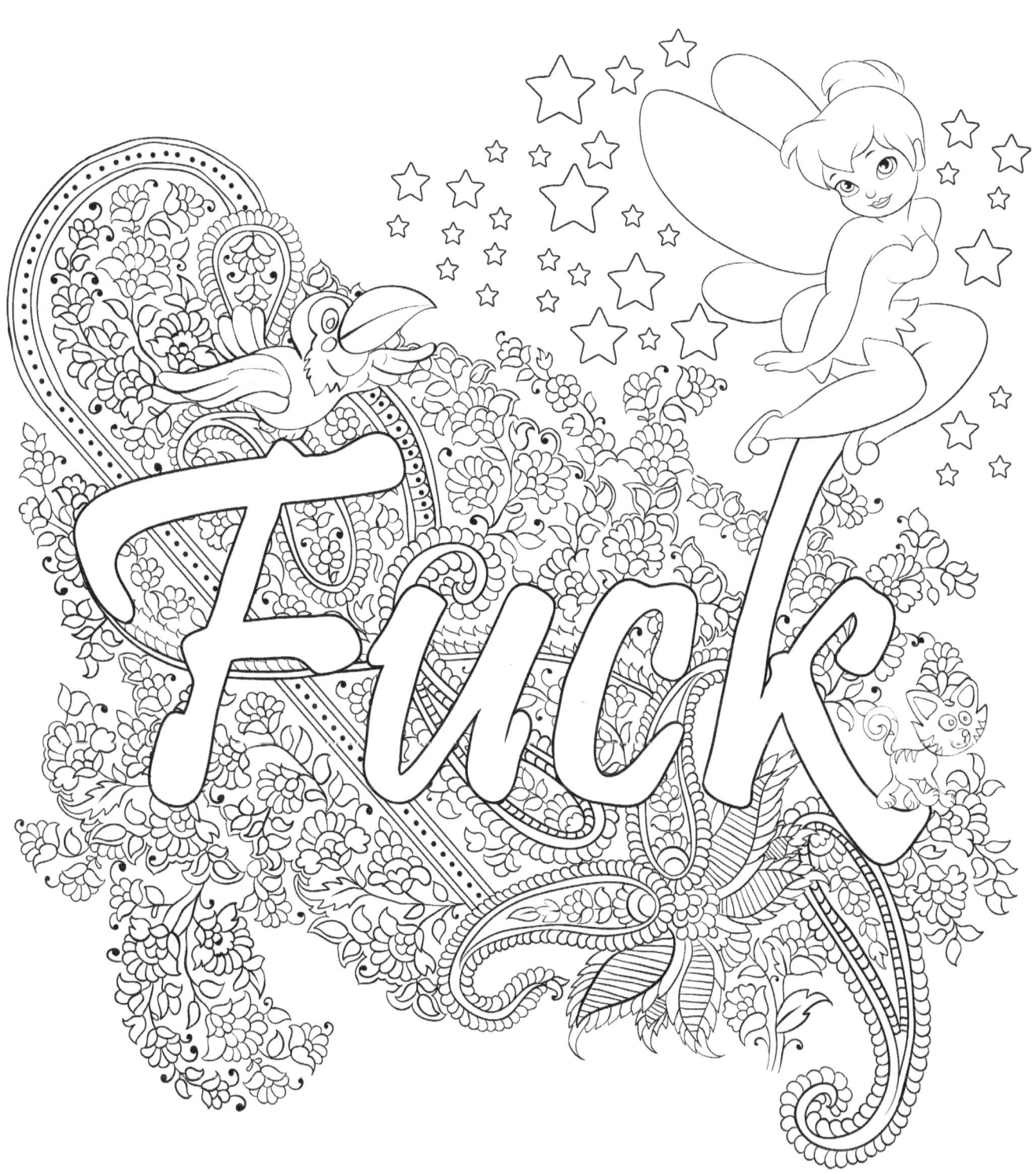

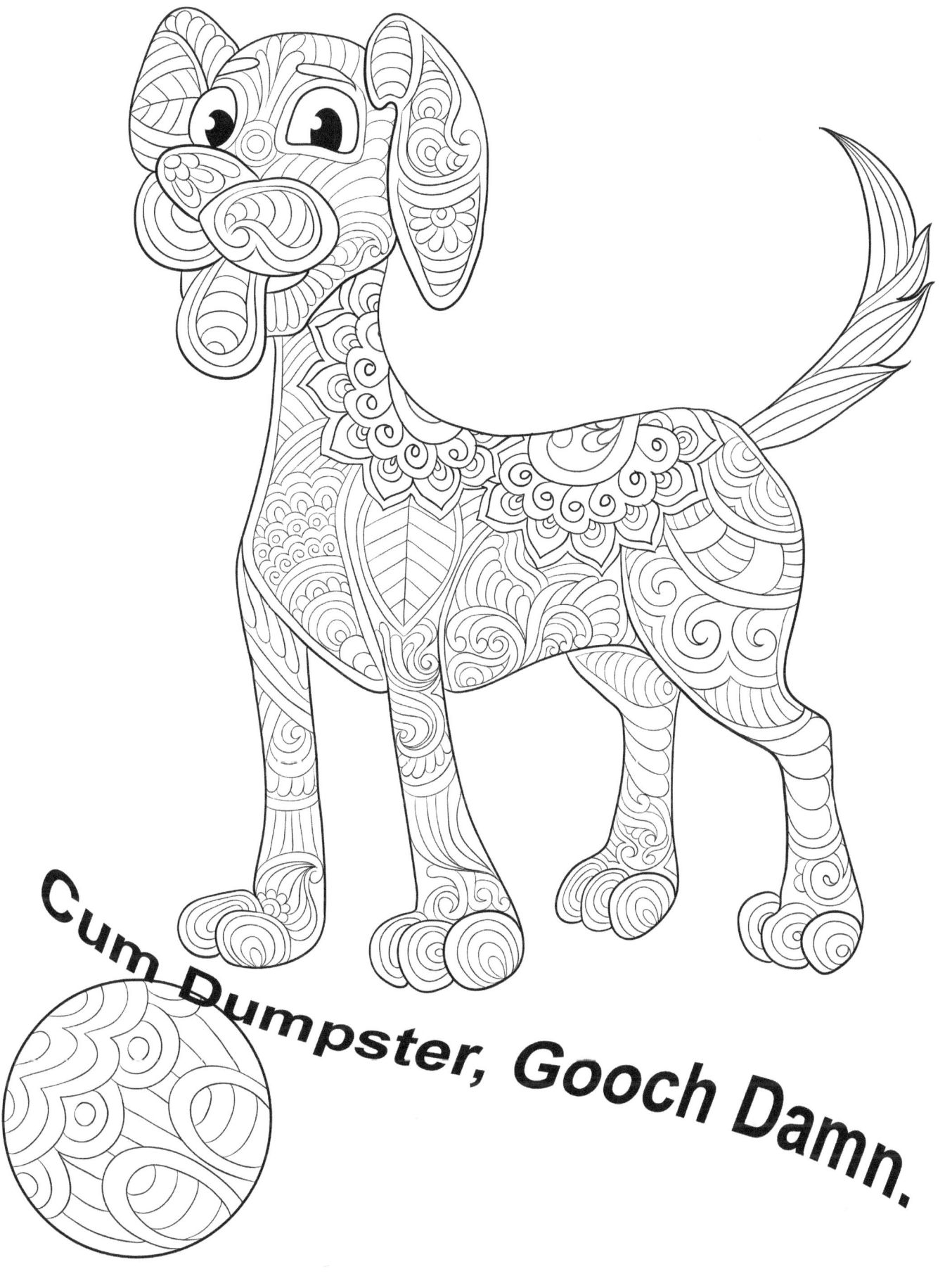

Cum Dumpster, Gooch Damn.

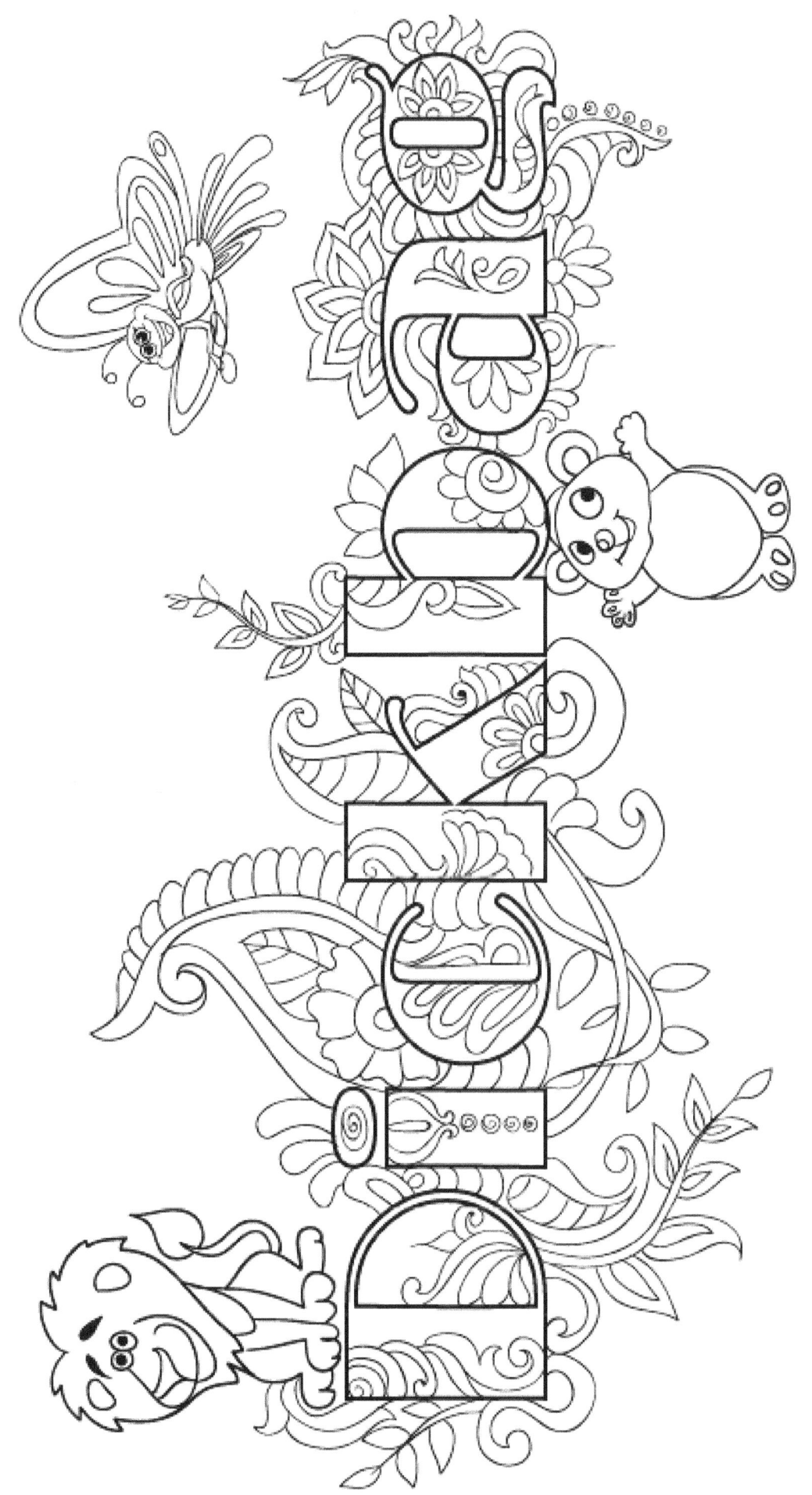

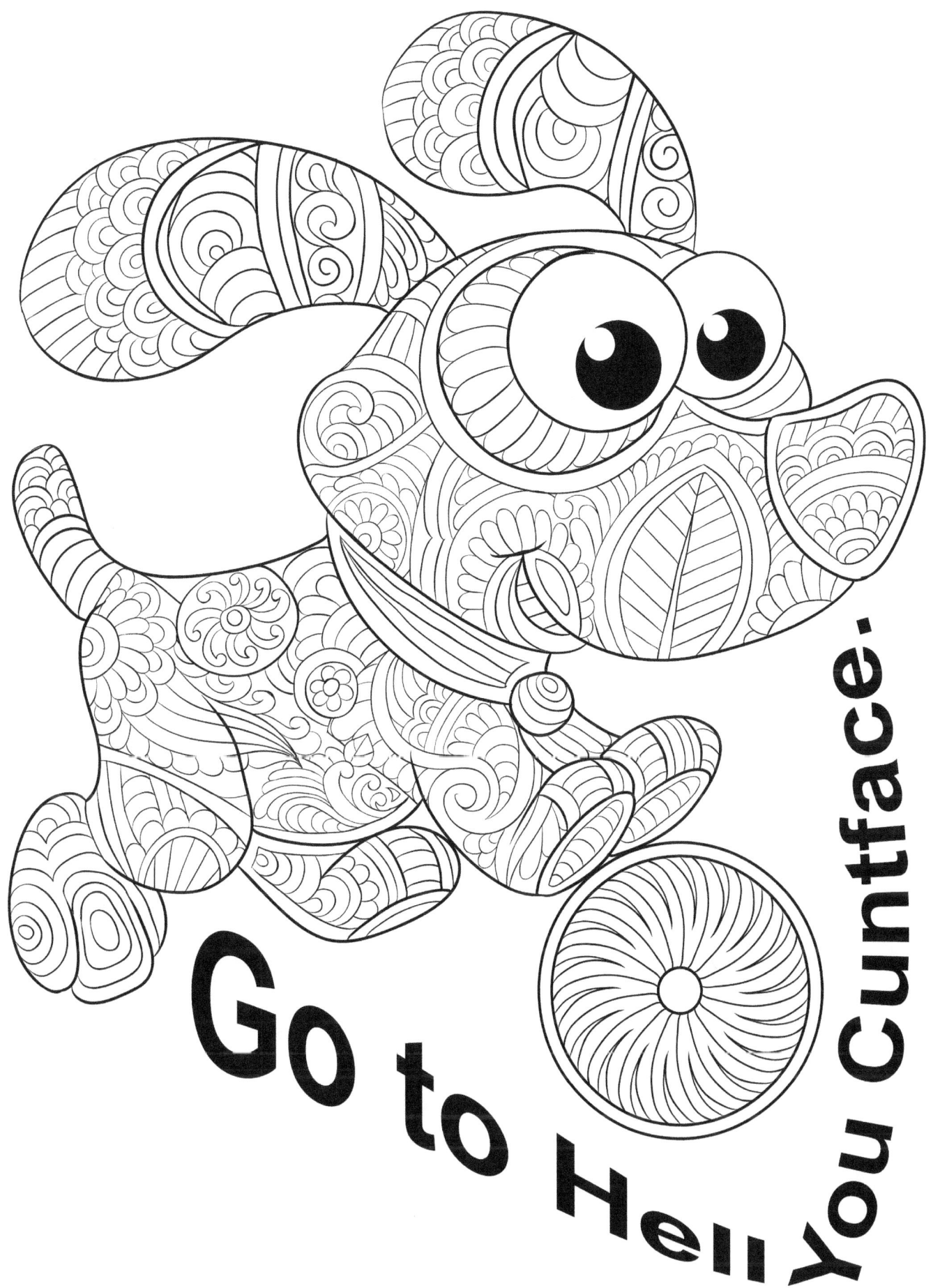

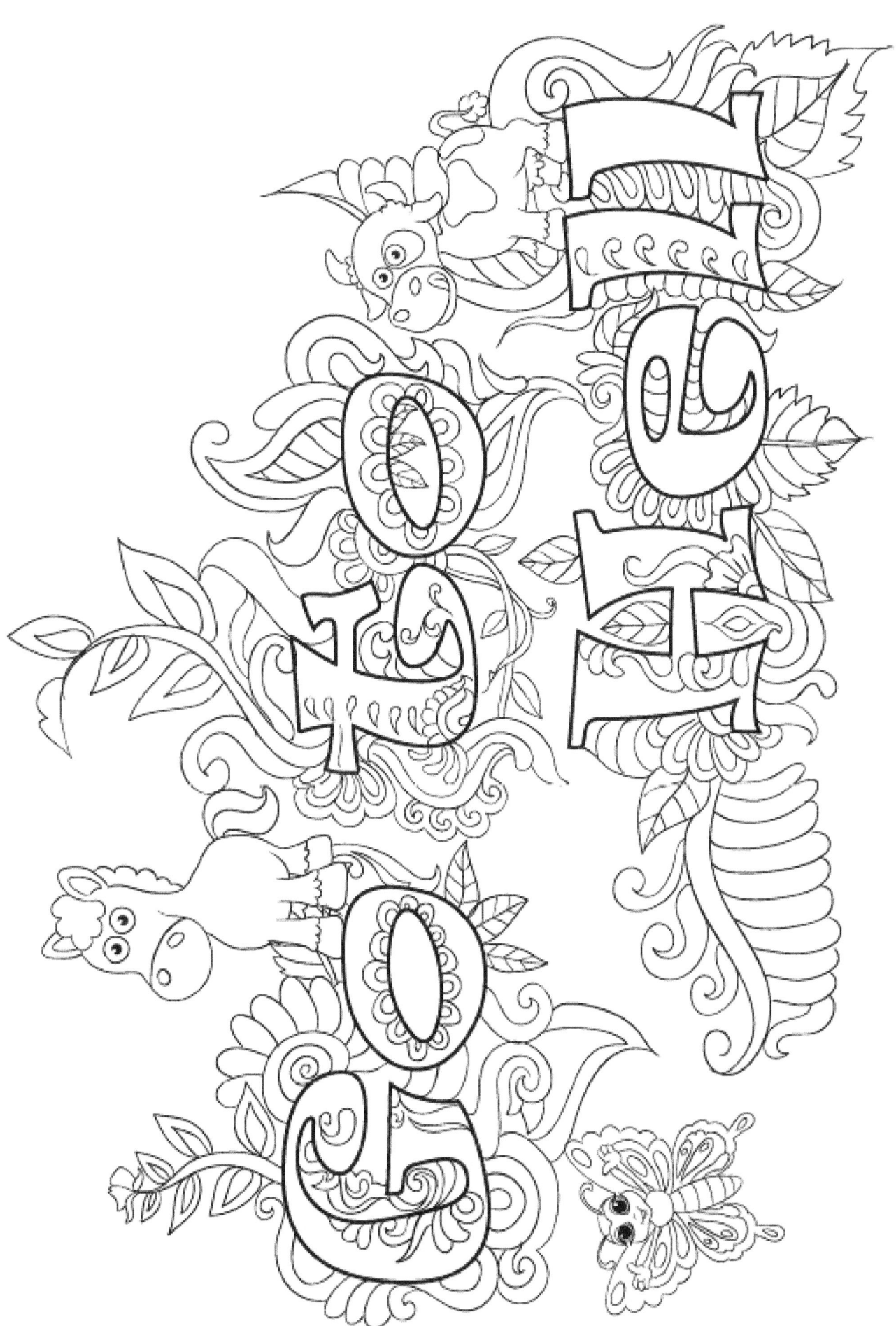

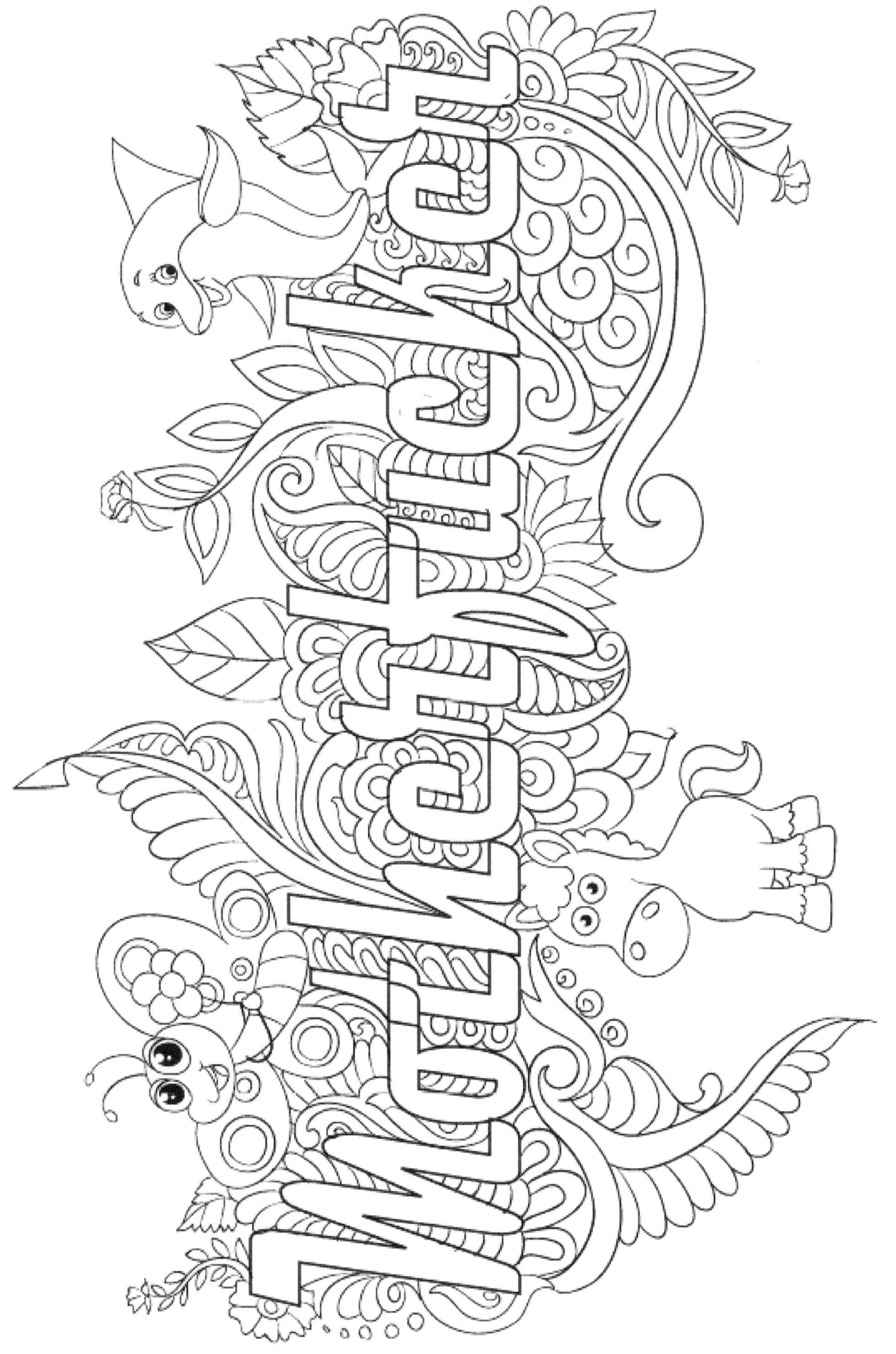

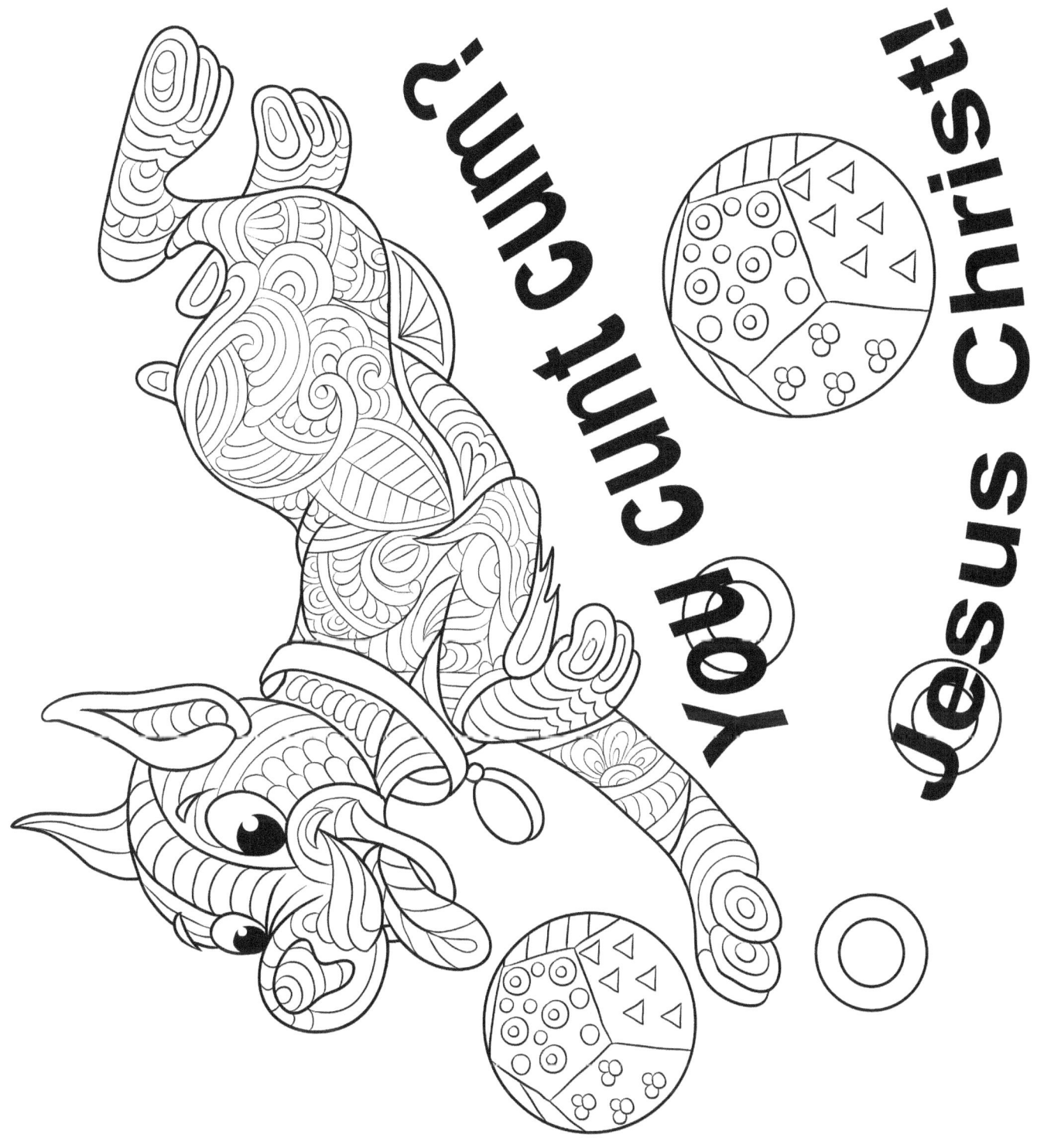

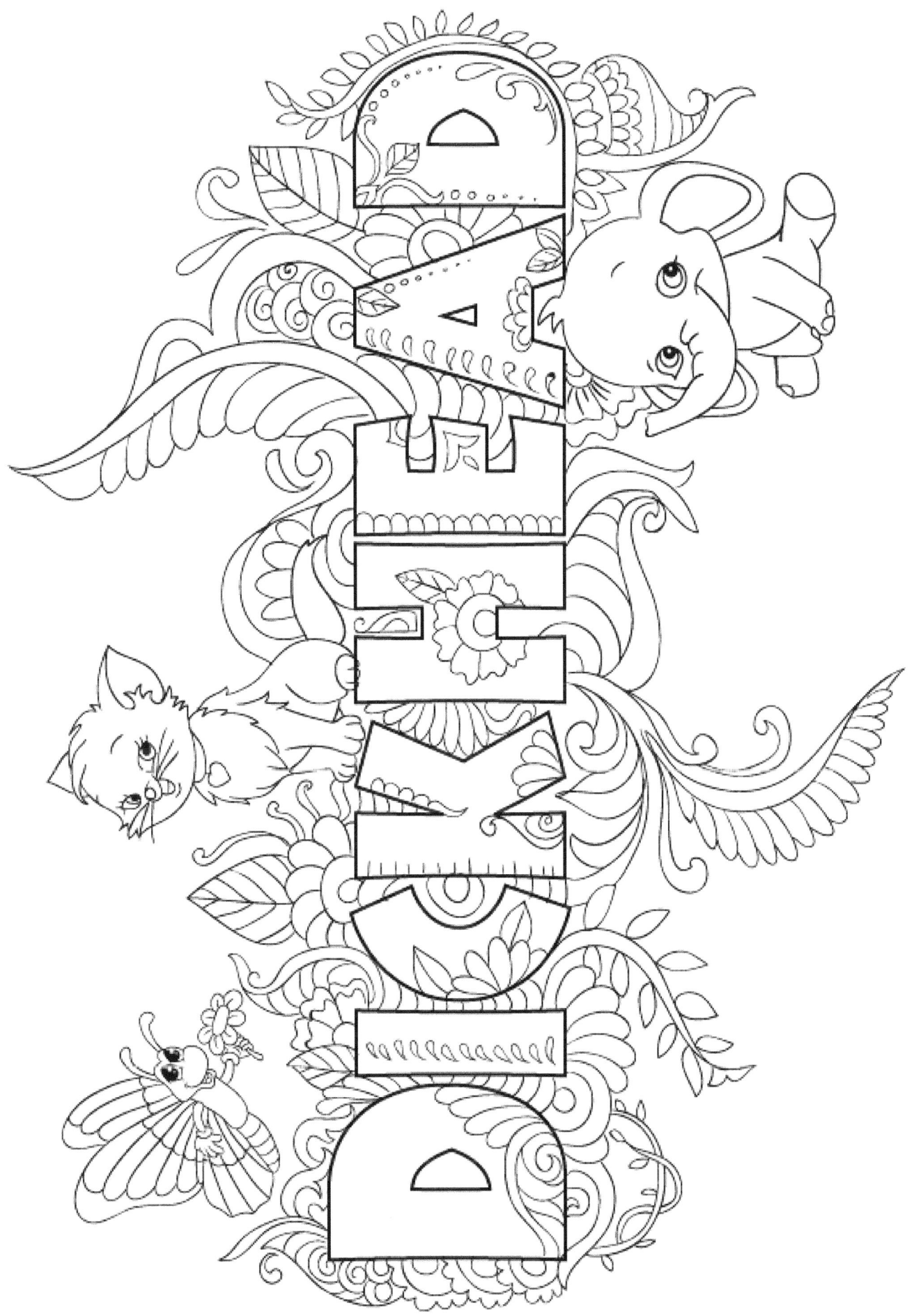

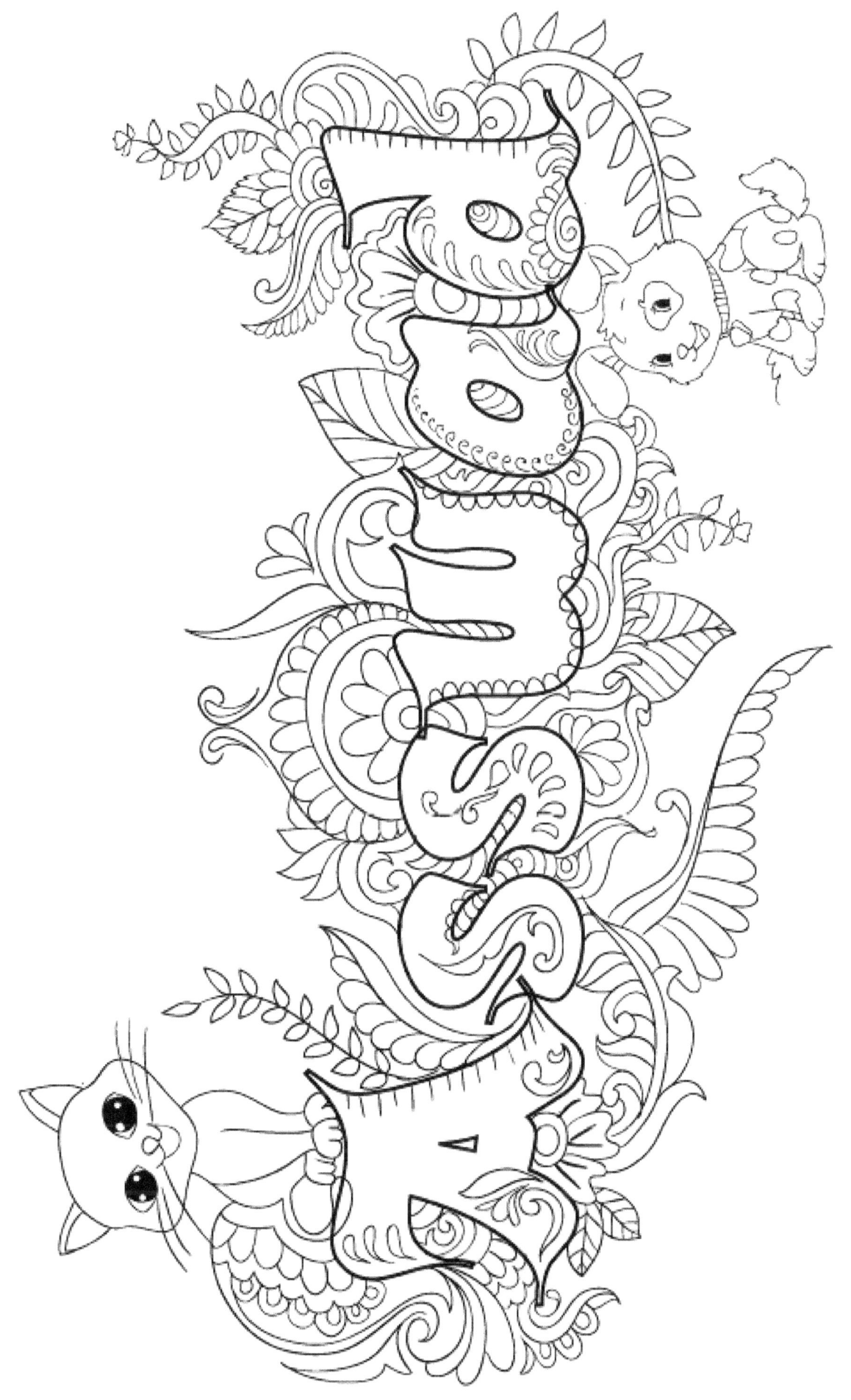

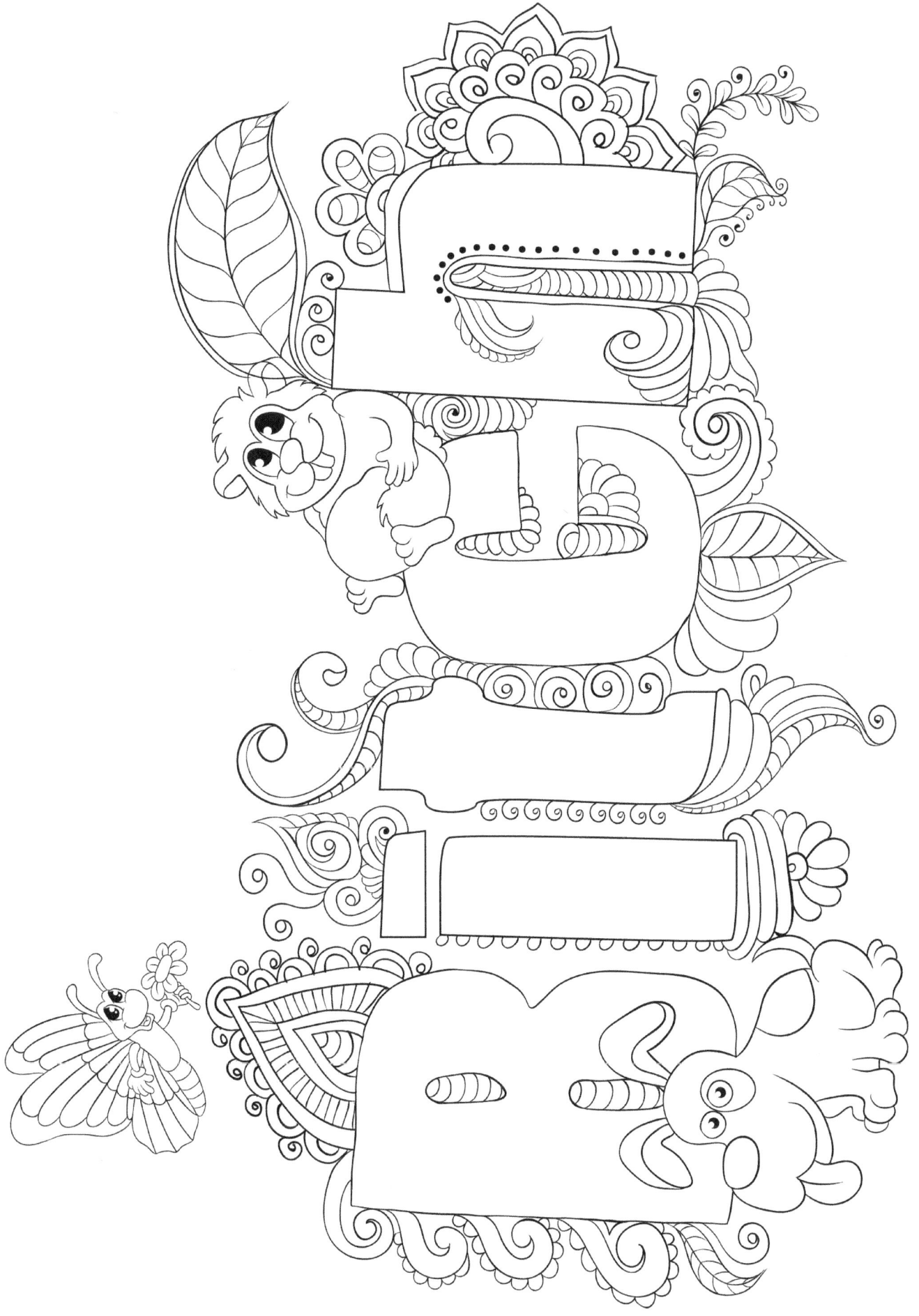

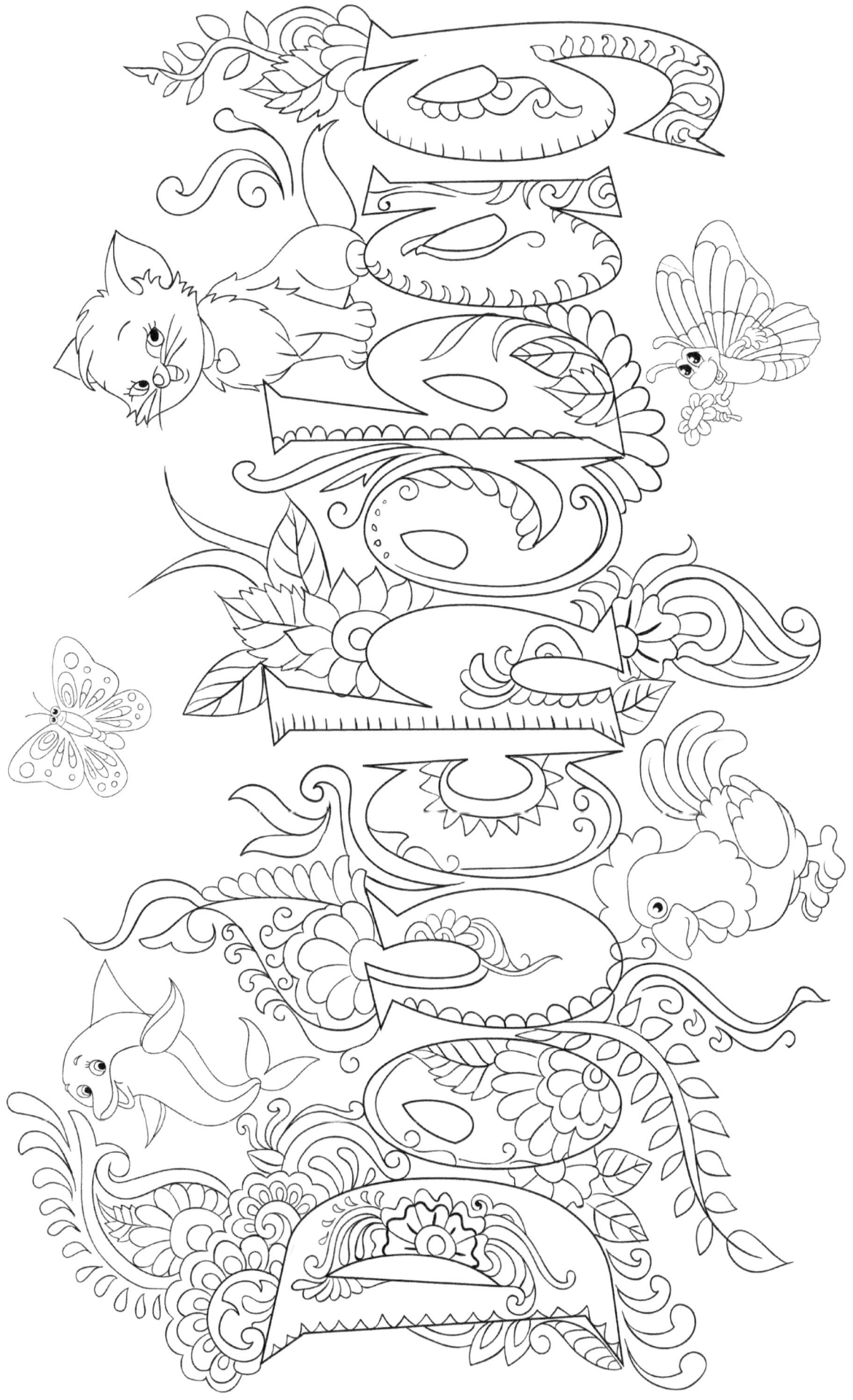

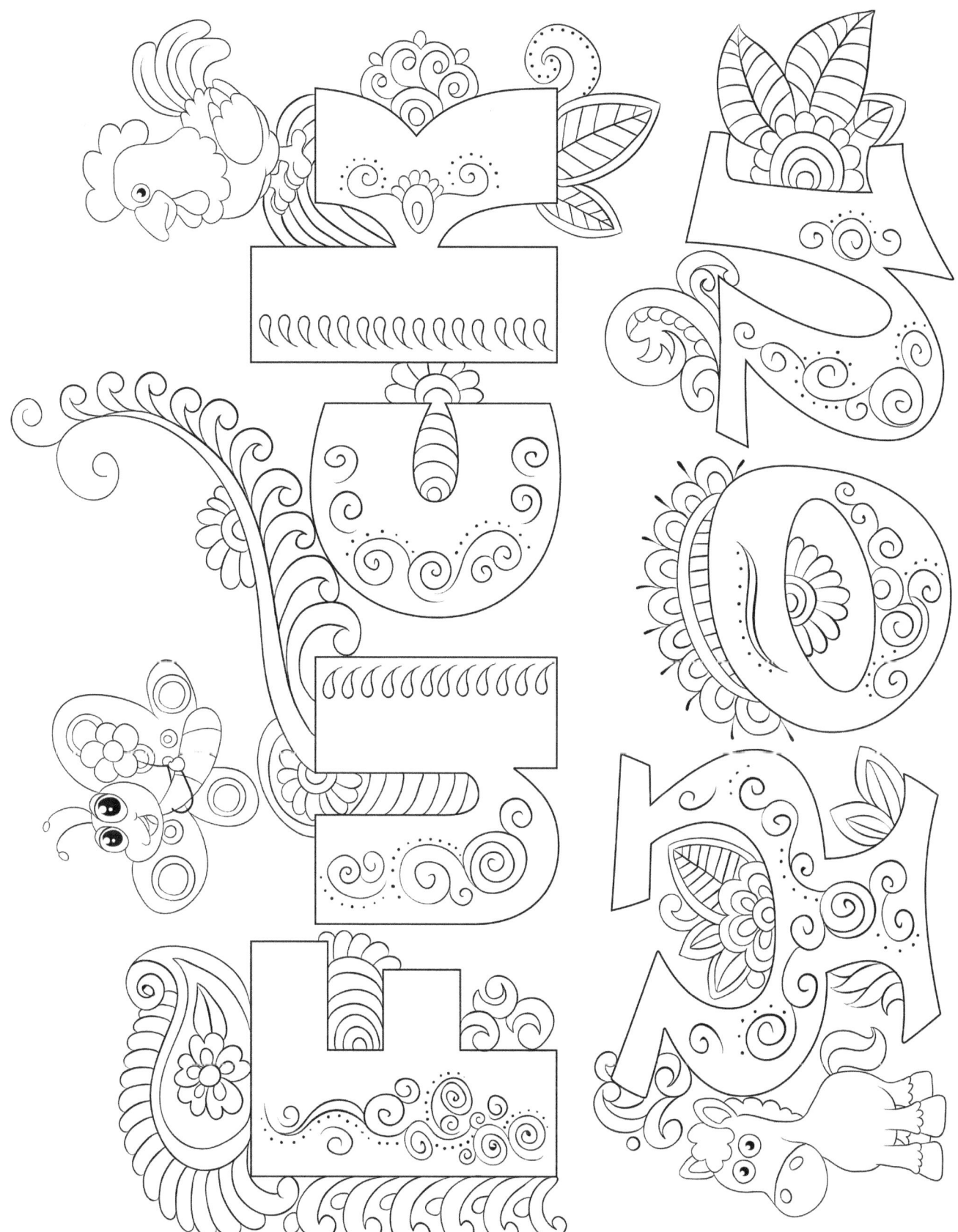

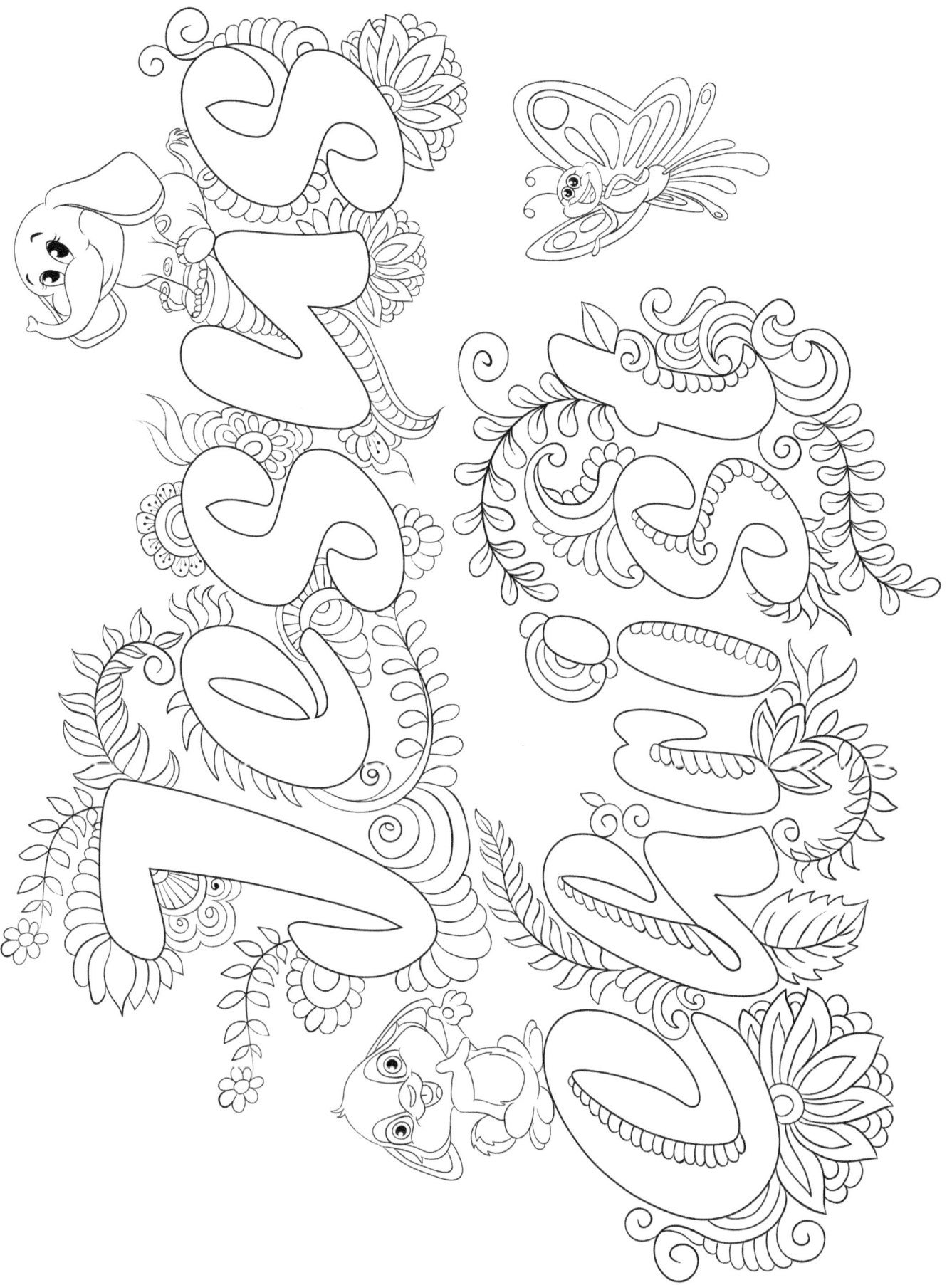

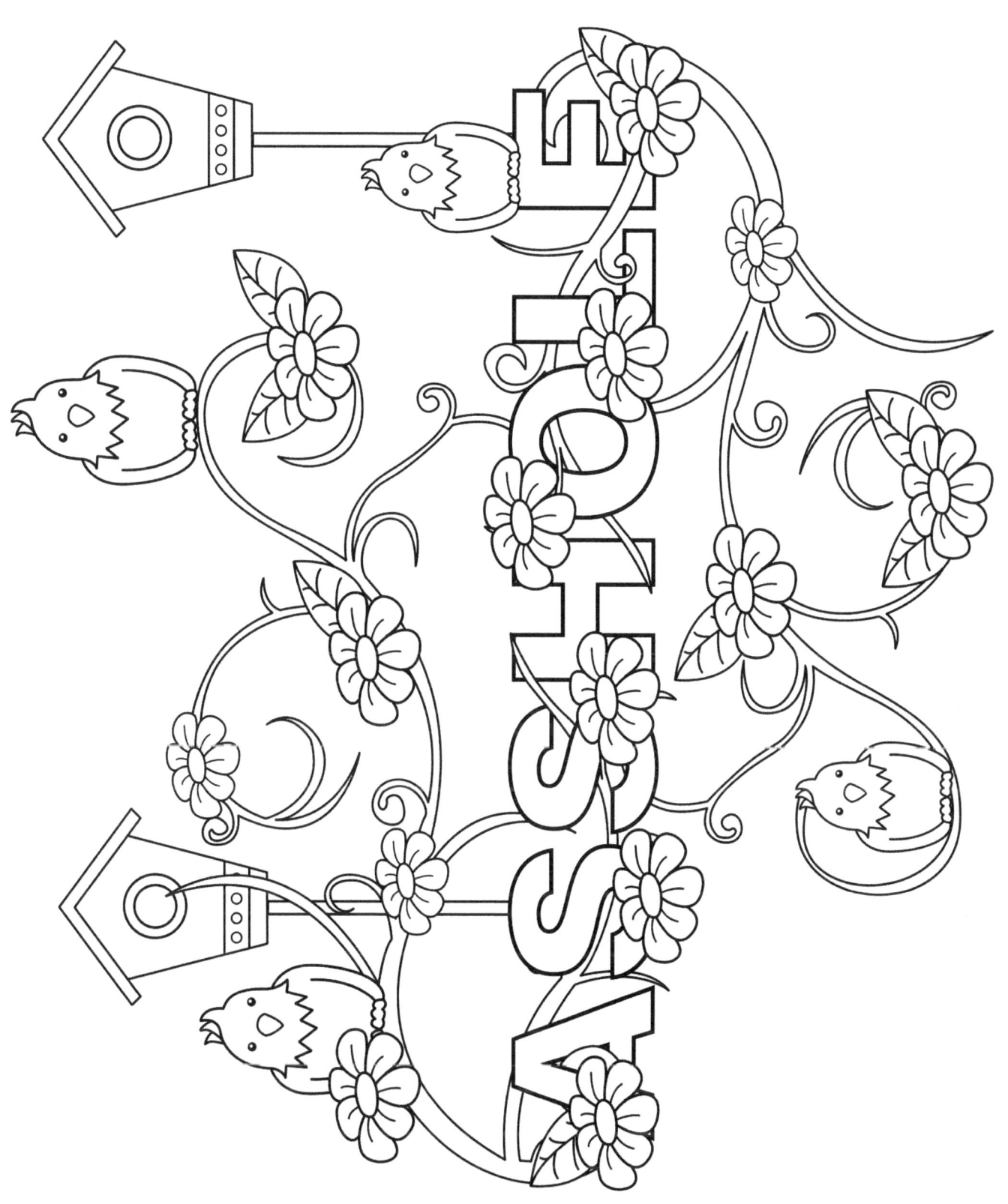

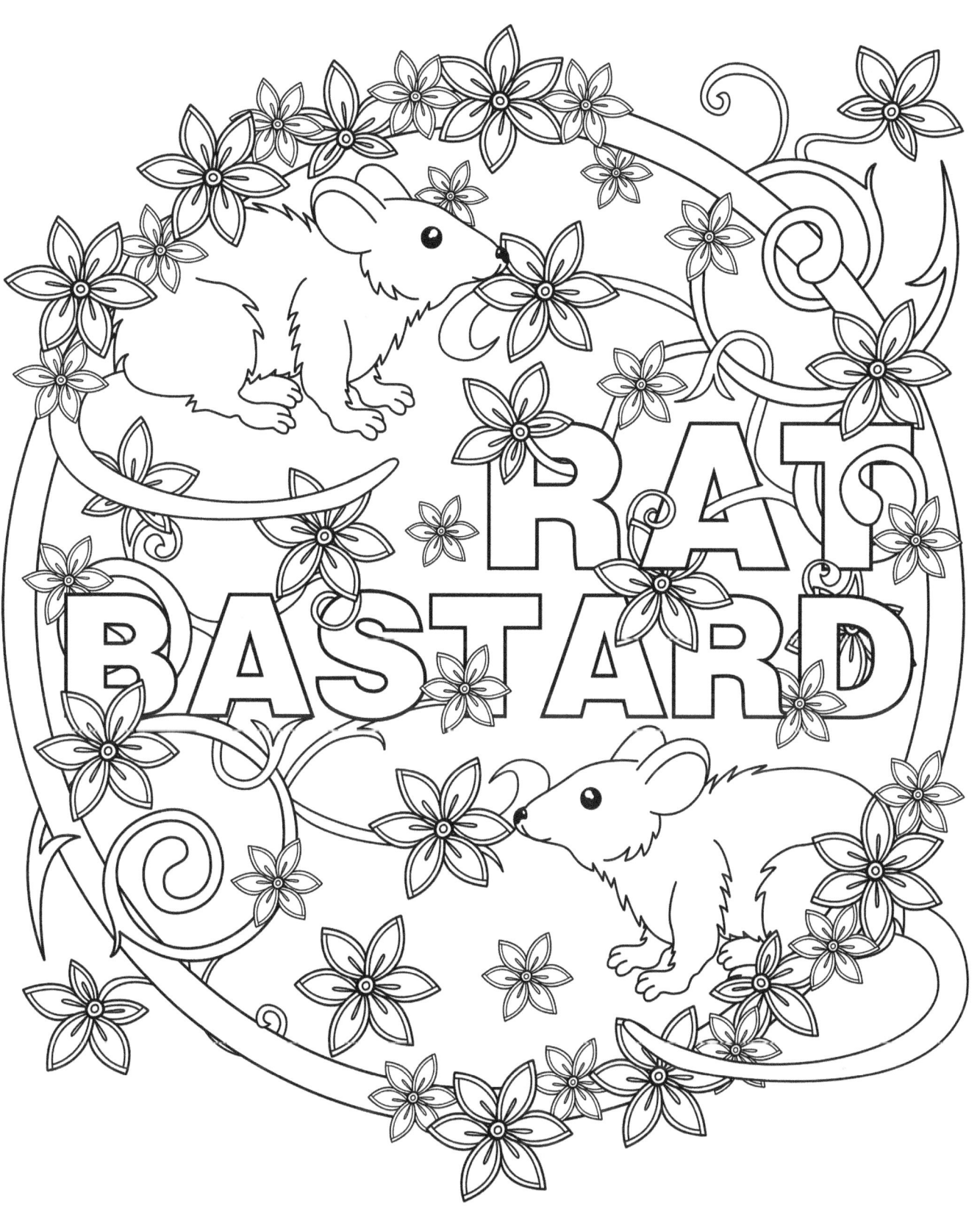

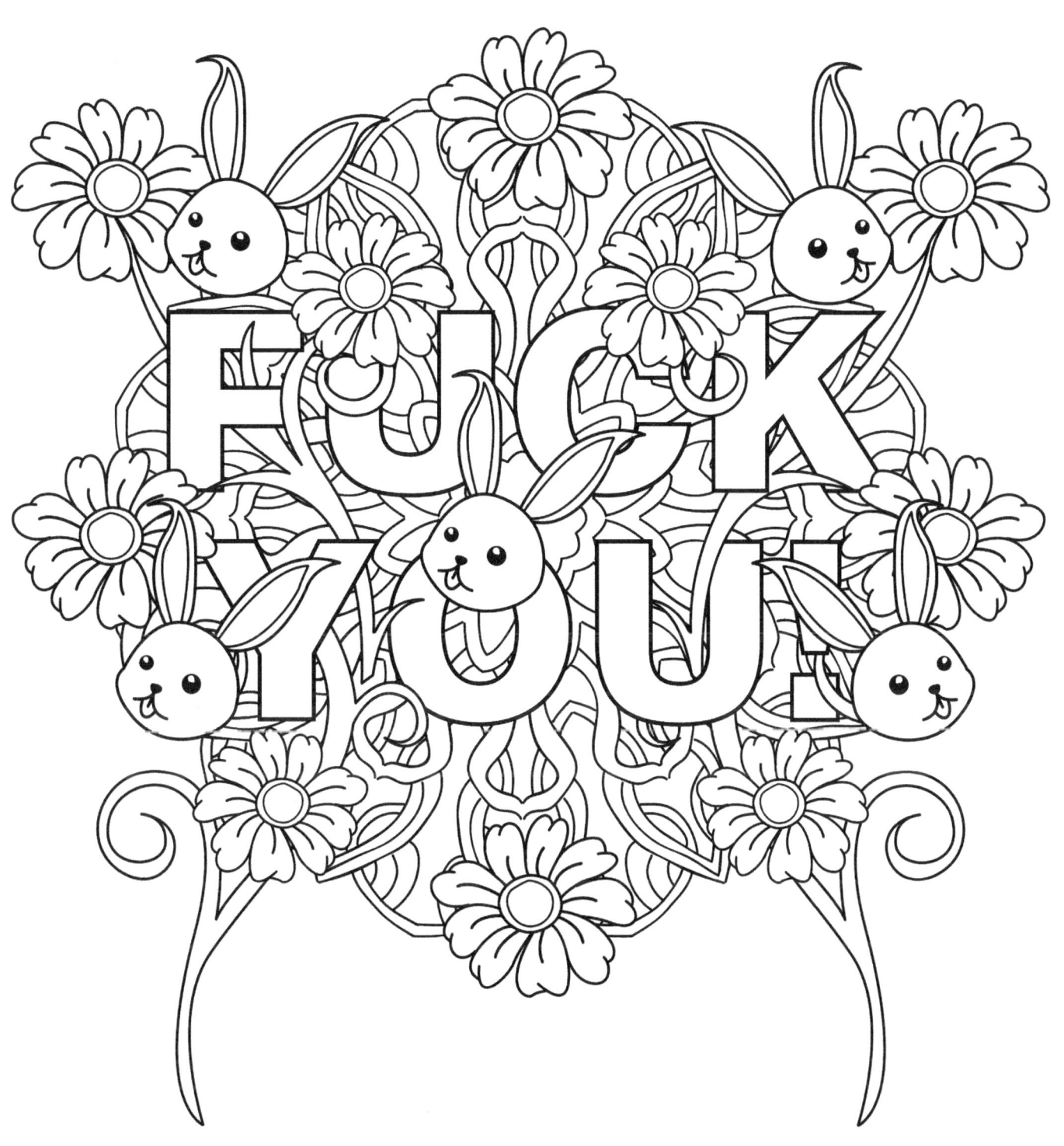

www.ingramcontent.com/pod-product-compliance
Lightning Source LLC
Chambersburg PA
CBHW080641190526
45169CB00009B/3451